Sandhurst Occasion

No 16

NATO and the Responsibility to Protect: Conference Proceedings

Edited by

Alicia Welland

Central Library

Royal Military Academy Sandhurst

2013

Introduction

This paper is a summary of a day-long event held as part of an ESRC-funded seminar series on 'NATO after Afghanistan'. This seminar was held at the Royal Military Academy Sandhurst on 5 June 2013 and discussed 'NATO and the Responsibility to Protect'.

The structure of the seminar was as follows:

Panel 1: The Antecedents of R2P (Responsibility to Protect)

- NATO's Balkan interventions
- African Interventions and Non-interventions

Panel 2: The development of R2P

- The politics of R2P
- R2P and International Law

Panel 3: Libya – precedent/model for future R2P military interventions?

- Military planning and command for alliance interventions: the Libya experience
- Challenges and controversies of the Libya intervention

Panel 4: Syria – a suitable case for intervention?

- Political and strategic obstacles to intervening in Syria
- Syria: the case for intervention

Final Roundtable: Future directions for R2P

The meeting was held under the Chatham House Rule and the views expressed are those of the participants. No names are therefore attributed to any of the points made in the open discussions. Also, where requested the identity of panel speakers has been withheld. This paper is intended to serve as an aide-mémoire to those who took part and to provide a general summary for others.

Panel 1: The Antecedents of R2P

NATO's Balkan interventions
Dr Niall Mulchinock (University College Cork)

This speaker examined the political, legal and strategic controversies that attended the NATO interventions in Bosnia and Kosovo. To conclude he looked at the subsequent lessons learned from these interventions and the debates that they gave rise to.

With regard to political controversies the speaker began by discussing the evolving NATO member state positions. Four states in particular have shaped NATO policy towards the Western Balkans over the last 20 years: US, Britain, France and Germany. Medium sized member states such as Denmark and Turkey also made a significant contribution to the 'use of force' debates during the Bosnian war in the early 1990s. There was some conflict between the positions of these key member states. During the Bosnian war there was a clear divide between European and American positions on using force (The European rejection of 'lift and strike'). This significantly undermined NATO as it was being publicly criticised for its inaction to curb acts of ethnic cleansing in Bosnia. There was therefore a more determined will to act in a unified manner when further instabilities broke out in Kosovo and Macedonia.

Some tensions escalated between NATO member states and NATO commanders during the peace enforcement missions. The disturbances in Kosovo in 2000 and 2004 exemplified these underlying difficulties. The speaker argued that NATO member states should also be criticised for not undertaking a greater range of roles during the early years of the IFOR and SFOR missions in Bosnia.

The early collective allied response to curbing ethnic hostilities in Macedonia in the early 2000s showed that member states had learned much from errors committed previously in the 1990s. The only major political controversy in the Macedonia case study related to a delay in the transfer of authority from NATO to the EU where these brief stabilisation missions were concerned.

The second element of political controversy related to the role of the NATO Secretary-General. The position of the NATO Secretary-General has been modified as a result of NATO's Balkan interventions. Dr Manfred Wörner made a significant contribution to NATO's post cold war development during his tenure as NATO Secretary-General from 1988 to 1994. Importantly, he urged an early allied military intervention in Bosnia through a variety of speeches he gave in 1993. In the latter stages of the Bosnian war and the crisis in Kosovo, Willy Claes and Dr. Javier Solana were operating in different political contexts as Secretary-Generals. There was a more collective will to act on the part of the allies in 1995 and 1999.

The third source of political controversy indentified is NATO's relations with international and regional organisations. Effective co-operation between NATO and other international organisations has been a central component of the international community's engagement with the Western Balkans. This process of co-operation has been adapted and modified to take account of previous mistakes made primarily in the 1990s. The UN/NATO relationship during the Bosnian war could be criticised for an inability by both organisations to develop common objectives. The dual-key mandate clearly didn't work as both organisations had different aims. NATO's operation 'Deny Flight' could be defined as being an experimental post Cold War peace enforcement operation while the UNPROFOR force on the ground was an outdated Cold War peacekeeping mission.

More effective co-operation came in the late 1990s and early 2000s during the Kosovo and Macedonian interventions. An evolving strategic partnership has developed between the EU and NATO where the Western Balkans are concerned. This has set precedents for further EU/NATO co-operation in Afghanistan and in the volatile Gulf of Aden region.

Having assessed the political controversies, the speaker turned to the legal issues surrounding the Balkan interventions. In the case of the NATO intervention in Bosnia in 1995 the legal controversies surrounding it weren't particularly obvious. The existence of the dual-key mandate along with the evolving relationship between UN and NATO commanders gave a certain legality to Operation Deliberate Force. On the other hand, Operation Allied Force in 1999 was a more controversial operation. Yet, despite this controversy the speaker argued that Operation Allied Force was a necessary military intervention due to the threat of a spread of conflict.

The speaker tackled the strategic controversies of the interventions. He pointed out that arguments against military intervention were made during the early stages of the Bosnian war due to the topography and geography of the country. It was also noted that a quagmire-like situation could develop if there was a Western military intervention in Bosnia

(General Colin Powell). However, these views were criticised by other retired senior military officers (General Sir Anthony Farrar-Hockley). Another strategic element is that in the Kosovo crisis in 1999 the air war lasted longer than was expected.

To conclude, the speaker assessed the general lessons learned by NATO. Firstly, there is a need to intervene militarily if necessary in the early stages of a conflict depending on the underlying factors on the ground. NATO learned a valuable lesson from its experience of the Bosnian conflict and these mistakes would not be repeated when the Kosovo crisis flared up in 1998. This lesson also impacted heavily on the EU through its development of a common European Security and Defence Policy at the end of the 1990s.

The second lesson is the need to co-operate effectively with other regional and international organisations. The early years of the IFOR and SFOR missions in Bosnia demonstrated NATO's determination to stick to prescribed aims and goals. It was only in the latter years of the SFOR mission in Bosnia that NATO began to adopt new and innovative roles such as defence reform.

Thirdly the speaker identified the need to integrate the states of the Western Balkans into the European and Euro-Atlantic institutions for their future security and stability. As of 2013 Albania, Croatia and Slovenia are fully integrated into NATO's political and military structures. Montenegro and Macedonia are the next likely states to join NATO. The political situations in Bosnia, Kosovo and Serbia mean that their prospects could be stalled in the short to medium term.

In comparing NATO's interventions in the Balkans to those in Afghanistan and Libya, the speaker identified certain similarities. In both instances you had dogmatic dictators who were persecuting their own people and the duration of these operations also lasted longer than expected.

African Interventions and Non-interventions
Lt Col[retd] Peter McCutcheon (Royal Military Academy Sandhurst)

The speaker argued for a 'pragmatic intervention model' rather than a moral intervention model, and that collective action theory tends to govern intervention efficiency rather than morality. He identified a need for efficiency when approaching humanitarian intervention, as without this legitimacy will suffer (efficiency breeds legitimacy).

Collective action theory argues that when a group is concerned with the provision of public goods it can produce certain behaviours within that group (see work by Olson and Searle). There are policy entrepreneurs who dominate debate and free riders that exploit this ('free-riding' on the efforts of others). Inaction becomes an art form as free riders become stakeholders and therefore acquire perceived and actual rights to be consulted. This breeds inaction, which in turn breeds inefficient response in a multi-actor environment. Therefore, the negative effects of collective action are threefold; difficulty in accepting agreed purpose, presence of spoilers who may delay or block the intervention, and jointery (there may be an issue of national policy trumping international policy once engaged).

These malign effects of collective action have a variety of impacts. Firstly, outside of Africa the result is 'bipolar disorder'/'clever cowardice'. Secondly, there can be selfish seclusion by the OAU/AU (internal to Africa). Thirdly, multi-actor coalitions are rendered ineffective if a rapid response is required. With too many red lines individual actors can become frustrated, resulting in unilateral action or action by small bilateral groups.

A consent gap exists between the degree of violence in a state as it moves towards a crisis and the international reaction. The external response always lags behind internal events, with clever cowardice allying itself to selfish seclusion. The search for an acceptable trigger breeds increasing frustration to the point where collective action theory dictates individual action to cross the consent gap (this is usually at a point way past when morality would dictate action).

To summarise, the pattern of behaviours for collective action is as follows: 'collective indifference' to 'selective engagement' to 'collective failure' to 'independent engagement'.

In the case of Africa the speaker cited 3 key intervention triggers or intervention justifications: The historical imperative to intervene is due to colonial disengagement, the hegemonic obligation, and lastly, humanitarianism (which he argued comes a poor third).

In terms of UK intervention is Africa, other than Sierra Leone there has been a fairly limited degree of engagement with some anti-mutiny and Non-combatant Evacuation Operations (NEOs) in the Congo and Rhodesia. Therefore the UK has little experience and little to offer when considering intervention in Africa. In contrast, the French record in Africa presents an example of pragmatic intervention theory in action. The French conducted a long, deliberate and pragmatic withdrawal from empire through a policy of preferential, self-interested disengagement based on cold pragmatism and conducted with a free hand. The French threw off collective action theory under De Gaulle.

In the French retreat from empire 1945-90 the use of 'diplomacy of the Jaguar' is evident. D'Estaing then shifted to an openly interventionist policy in the 1970s, while Mitterrand self imposed restraints in 1981. There was a loss of confidence in 1990-96; the end of conscription meant a smaller regular army, the public were increasingly lukewarm to the concept of intervention and there had also been French involvement in Rwanda in 1994 (the French held doors open for génocidaires to escape justice, demonstrating naked self-interest). However, from 1996-2007 there was a return to protection. Here NEOs plus defence accords are a product of expediency. Expediency then turned from a vice into a virtue. Since 2007 there has been a search for partnership, with a coupling of financial imperatives to determination to influence. Operation SERVAL in Mali underlines this.

To conclude, the speaker argued that efficiency breeds legitimacy. Pragmatism dictates that the most efficient tool for bridging the consent gap is via single or bi-lateral action, often in the face of spoilers. For example, the Kodio diamond miners in Sierra Leone, who were in the hands of the RUF were 'liberated' by a small, agile and powerful force in an operation that covered 250kms in 2 days in June 1995. This was not conducted by UN forces but by Executive Outcomes. R2P needs to find a way of delivering effect and the speaker argued that it needs to be coldly pragmatic if it is to work.

Discussion

- French operation in Mali: sums up how French would like us to do business. It is argued that a single force on the ground best delivers effect.

- It is noted that humanitarian intervention is too late too often.

- Comment from the floor that pragmatism and morality do not necessarily have to be traded off (consider the Just War principles).

- It is questioned whether NATO is simply a tool of member states.
  - o Consideration of the tensions between member states.
  - o It is added that we should not underestimate the importance of individuals and their influence. For example, the role of the Secretary General in influencing NATO member states (Solana was a major influence over Kosovo in 1998).

- The importance of the impact and influence of public sentiment on foreign policy is taken into account.

- Where does it end?
  - o The importance of the legal implications of the kind of pragmatic interventions the second speaker discussed (using the French approach to intervention as an example) is mentioned. It was suggested that a problem might arise with a cold pragmatic approach, as it would set a precedent for this kind of intervention. If this were the case then it would make room for other countries like China to intervene in the same manner.

- It is argued that problems emerge when we try to look to regional powers in the case of Africa. For example, Nigeria's place as a regional power is no longer pronounced due to its current inward looking policy. South Africa also is not stepping up as major power.

Summary:
- The importance of intervening in the early stages of a conflict and effective cooperation with regional and international organisations are pointed out as key lessons from the Balkan interventions.
- It is argued that we need to consider a more pragmatic approach to intervention, with efficiency as a focus, moving away from

---

Panel 2: The Development of R2P

The politics of R2P

Dr Aidan Hehir (University of Westminster)

Humanitarian intervention represents a particularly divisive topic for international relations, despite its recognised importance.

To consider the origins of R2P the speaker began by looking at the actions of the UN Security Council in the 1990s. Actions tended to be inconsistent, (Rwanda vs. Haiti) and were dependent on the consent of the P5. It is this lack of full P5 consent that made the Kosovo intervention "illegal but legitimate".

The UN Charter Chapter VII states that: '[The] Security Council...may take such action by air, sea, or land forces as may be necessary to maintain or restore international peace and security. Such action may include demonstrations, blockade, and other operations by air, sea, or land forces.' At this point the speaker questioned whether 'restoring international peace and security' constitutes humanitarian intervention. There is a danger here that intervention is not based on the scale of the tragedy but on national interests.

R2P signifies the responsibility to prevent, react and possibly rebuild. It sets out the internal responsibility of states towards their own people as well as the external responsibility of the international community (towards people suffering within states "unable" or "unwilling" to help them).

The speaker noted that states agree on the following five principles with regard to R2P:

- The African Union's 2000 Constitutive Act was a significant development in the evolution of R2P;
- Prevention is a key component of R2P;
- R2P is not a new legal principle (it is a restatement of existing laws);
- R2P only applies to the four crimes listed in the World Summit Outcome Document; genocide, war crimes, ethnic cleansing and crimes against humanity.
- R2P's efficacy is contingent on the mobilization of political will.

There has been praise for R2P in regard to the new momentum it added to the debate on humanitarian intervention. It binds states to internal and external commitments as well as formally recognising "conditional sovereignty". It has also been lauded for being realistic and feasible (as it does not require significant change) and for bringing clarity by outlining the "four crimes".

Yet, the speaker also identified that R2P's introduction has been tempered with criticism. It is felt by some that R2P can be construed as a "western" plot or that it adds nothing new in terms of laws, institutions and competencies. In light of the latter it is also noted that R2P exaggerates the power of shame to compel action, and leaves the primacy of the P5 within the Security Council unchanged.

R2P, despite its praise is argued to have little to say on key military questions such as who will be doing the intervening, and where the troops will come from. For example, in Darfur, a force was mandated to intervene, but few states wanted to get involved.

Sources of pressure to take action can come from the UN Secretary-General, Media/Non-Governmental Organisations, Domestic/Global Civil Society and individual states. However, in terms of implementation we are still left with the problem of who decides, the UNSC must sanction action, yet the P5 are not bound by 'duty' or 'obligation'. National governments then choose when to invoke R2P, with intervention dependent on the political will of each P5 member (scale of violence can become secondary to the primary concerns of Russia/China).

The speaker moved to discussing the Libyan 2011 intervention. UN Secretary-General Ban Ki-Moon said of the intervention in Libya in 2011 that: "By now it should be clear to all that R2P has arrived".

The 2011 intervention was mandated on the basis of Chapter VII. The intervention in Libya could be considered a unique case of success due to the strong coincidence of factors. For example, the Arab League was in support of intervention in Libya and Libya lacked the strong regional allies of Syria.

Despite the statement of Ban Ki-Moon set out above there was no mention of international R2P in Resolution 1973, nor was there any mention of R2P during Security Council debates or by Obama, Cameron and Sarkozy. Therefore there is little evidence that any of the P5 acted out of respect of R2P.

There are several ongoing controversies in relation to R2P highlighted by the speaker. Firstly the selectivity of intervention, the speaker questioned where R2P was when the GCC intervened in Bahrain. Secondly, from the lessons learnt in Libya there is the issue of whether Russia and China will ever abstain again given the Libyan "mandate-stretch". Thirdly the issue of institutional reform: Does Russia and China's policy towards Syria demonstrate R2P's ineffectiveness? Lastly the speaker warned of the looming multi-polarity: Is Brazil's "Responsibility While Protecting" evidence of a new opposition amongst the BRIC (Brazil, Russia, India, China) countries and others?

R2P and International law
Professor Steven Haines (University of Greenwich)

The speaker began by outlining the legal controversy that generated R2P following the Kosovo conflict in terms of whether the intervention was legal. It was noted that one could argue that a justification for NATO intervention can be found within customary law, (the customary right of humanitarian intervention) which can then be counted in international law.

The counter argument to the above approach holds that there can be no 'customary right' that goes beyond the UN Charter. A justification needs to be looked for within treaty law and customary law. The problem lies in the use of a veto in the Security Council. If we look at the UN Charter you are required to have the assenting votes of all five members to have a binding resolution. However, at the same time, what the UN has practised has moved away from this. A custom has emerged that if members abstain rather than veto the resolution then it can still be passed with the majority assenting.

R2P in 2005 meant very little of what it is implied to mean today. In reality R2P has not had any profound impact on international law. There has been no treaty change or change to the UN Charter. The speaker also argued that it would be very surprising if a change were made to treaty law on the use of force as a result of R2P. For a change to be made in customary law you would need a significant change in state practice. However, this has not been the case with the recent pattern of not intervening on the basis of the responsibility to protect. Here, the speaker also argued that Libya was not an R2P operation.

In terms of the customary right to humanitarian intervention as mentioned above, R2P put an end to a debate on this rather than affirming it. The Responsibility to Protect affirms the decision making power of the Security Council. Therefore the customary right of intervention as discussed in relation to Kosovo is no longer applicable (there is little reference to a 'right to intervene' used in the Responsibility to Protect).

To conclude, the speaker argued that R2P has had no impact on law since 1999, as there have not been any changes in the sources of law (customary or treaty based). In legal terms we would still need to refer strictly to the UN Charter in assessing the legality of intervention.

Discussion:

- It was noted that there has been a shift in the nature of the environment (from R2P to the war on terror).
- A comment was made that R2P may have caused an important change in international thinking, in terms of rights of intervention (the notion that states can do whatever they want within their own boundaries has gone).
- The second speaker argued that the above was in place long before R2P. Instead, R2P acted to enforce the notion that the UN Security Council had the decision making power.
- The first speaker added that it is a good thing that states can no longer do whatever they want in their own boundaries, but that R2P does not have the credit for this.
- As of yet, the debate on R2P and the change in international thinking has not changed the law.
- Comment from the floor that R2P relies on a western notion of state/sovereignty (and is therefore limited).

- The first speaker argued that it does not necessarily follow that R2P is euro centric just because it evolved from Europe. The notion of widespread state opposition to conditional sovereignty (beyond the West) is not necessarily true. We could also consider that the P5 might even attach a greater value to sovereignty than other states.

- Noted that R2P may have been blown off course by 9/11,

- The second speaker argued that although a perfectly logical legal argument was given to the then Prime Minister in the case of Iraq, this intervention may have stretched the notion of self-defence in legal terms. On the other hand, this speaker argued that Afghanistan was lawful.

- Noted that it is inconceivable that we would use military involvement to prop up an oppressive government.

- Comment was made that there is no evidence to link R2P to the Libyan intervention.

- There was a question on the desire for regime change vs. humanitarian justifications for intervention.

- The first speaker argued that there was no pre-existing plan for regime change in the case of Qaddafi

- One participant questioned whether chemical weapons should be distinguished from other forms of violence.

- U.S. awaiting 'right' evidence on use of chemical weapons in Syria. There is wariness that affirmation of the use of such weapons will draw them into intervention. Yet, ultimately, it is still the UNSC that will make the decision on intervention in Syria, rather than US action unilaterally.

Summary:
- The P5 are not bound by 'duty' or 'obligation', hence intervention is dependent on the political will of each member. There is also a selectivity of intervention.
- The Libyan intervention does not necessarily constitute an R2P intervention. It is argued that there is little evidence that the P5 acted out of respect for R2P.
- R2P has had no impact on law since 1999. No changes were made in customary or treaty law.

Panel 3: Libya - precedent/model for future R2P military interventions?

Military planning and command for alliance interventions: the Libya experience

A senior military officer from SHAPE

In the case of Libya, possible triggers for intervention include the Arab Spring and humanitarian catastrophe. There was a legal mandate present in the form of UNSCR 1973 ("All necessary measures to protect civilians under attack").

In terms of planning, the order of action/priority was as follows:

1. Humanitarian assistance
2. Arms embargo (UNSCR 1970 26TH Feb 11)
3. No Fly Zone (Arab league request 12th March 11).
4. No Fly Zone+

The planning phases for the Libyan operation moved extremely quickly in a matter of days rather than weeks. In terms of executing the operation there were no boots on the ground, with 100% precision guided weapons and targeting was ISR heavy. The prevention of civilian casualties was a key driver with difficulty found in de-confliction with anti-Qaddafi militias.

The speaker argued that North Atlantic Council meetings at NATO were concerned with protecting the people. Lessons were learnt from ISAF and applied here when involving member states. There appeared to be recognition of a need for parties to commit to something tangible, rather than solely having involvement in the discourse.

The lessons from Libya raise certain questions: Is this a future paradigm or a one-off? Do we need to consider western intervention in the wider Arab Spring?

Challenges and controversies of the Libya intervention
Dr Ian Davis (NATO Watch)

The speaker began by defining R2P and the nature of the Libyan intervention.

Responsibility to Protect represents a new norm to prevent and stop genocide, war crimes, ethnic cleansing and crimes against humanity. R2P is a political commitment and not a law (but founded upon international legal obligations). R2P builds on the concept of 'human security' challenging the longstanding principle of state sovereignty (it included responsibilities as well as rights). The mandate for the Libya intervention was provided by UNSCRs 1970 and 1973 and there was a coalition military intervention. Operation Unified Protector took place from the 31st March to the 31st October 2011. The mandate was to protect the population, enforce the arms embargo and impose a 'no-fly' zone. There were 26,000 sorties, 9,700 air strikes and <5,900 military and dual-use targets destroyed.

The speaker then questioned whether the use of force was appropriate. The ICISS (International Commission on Intervention and State Sovereignty) report produced in 2001 entitled 'The Responsibility to Protect', dealt with the question of when (if ever) it is appropriate for states to take coercive/military action against another state in order to prevent mass atrocities/ protect those at risk in that state. The report proposed four 'precautionary principles': right intention, last resort, proportional means and reasonable prospects. It also discussed two additional criteria: right authority and just cause.

One of the criticisms the speaker identified is that NATO may have conducted the operation too slowly. The reasons for intervention included fears of a mass exodus and Qaddafi's support of terrorists. The speaker ruled out oil as a motivation due to the West holding various oil contracts with Qaddafi (Intervention would therefore mean instability with regard to oil).

With regard to Operation Unified Protector and the questions it raised, the following issues were outlined by the speaker:

- Civilian protection or regime change - did the intervention go beyond the UN mandate? The speaker argued that this was the case in relation to UNSCR 1973. The forms of covert intervention used in the operation could be argued to have exceeded the mandate and there were accusations of duplicity in ignoring government checks and balances in covert military operations. We should also consider the possible limitations of the NATO consideration that only the removal of Qaddafi could provide long-lasting security.

- Did NATO do enough to prevent civilian deaths during the airstrikes? The recording of casualties could have been done differently to give a more accurate record.

- ICC indictments - help or hindrance? A positive element is that they may have a deterrent effect on other like-minded dictators. On the other hand, some critics argue that they prevented the option of a negotiated end to the war.

- Did the Libyan 'victory' result in post-conflict peace, stability and democratic rule? A key issue post-operation is the plethora of armed groups present in Libya. The speaker questioned whether enough has been done to disarm them and to prevent the looting of stockpiles. The impact of the conflict on Mali also merits further consideration.

- Was the impact on the R2P norm positive or negative? There is a difficulty in assessing the impact of Libya due to the individual nature of conflict. This individuality makes it hard for Libya to be used as a template for R2P intervention.

In terms of evaluation and lessons learnt, the speaker identified a need for further transparency and accountability by opening up the classified nature of many reports. The speaker also touched on two further key questions: whether NATO has emerged stronger or weaker and whether NATO should now make genocide a priority for its work.

To conclude, the speaker outlined a reform agenda for NATO and the future of R2P. The speaker identified the need to move beyond the 'war on terror' paradigm and establish an R2P committee/act for R2P. The speaker also recommended R2P training exercises and dialogue with Russia and China on NATO practices in these areas. Finally, as touched on earlier there is a need for NATO to undertake more accurate casualty recording.

Discussion:

- What was the relationship between rebels and NATO? The first speaker argued that there was no formal relationship between NATO planners and anti-Qaddafi rebels, targeting information came from the intelligence network.
- Civilian deaths from NATO airstrikes suggested to have been around 100.
- The first speaker mentioned a sense of 'family' within NATO. A question from the floor was whether this managed to override disputes/disagreements. The speaker argued there was a recognition that the alliance needed to be strong but with robust conversation.
- A participant questioned whether there is a need for a NATO initiative in disarming militia groups in Libya. It is considered whether security sector reform should have been in the initial planning for the intervention or whether NATO's help in this area should be requested by the new Libyan government.

- With regard to regional support, it is noted that there may be controversy surrounding Qatar's involvement due to the human rights issues in this country.

- A questioner asked at what point the shift in intention (from protect the people to regime change) occurred in the planning process. The first speaker replied that it was later on in the process that the shift in intention occurred rather than in the planning stages.

- A question was raised as to whether we would have been more effective with boots on the ground. The first speaker stated that this may have been the case but activity was limited to the air.

- Do we intervene if rebels are harming civilians? The first speaker argued that from a NATO perspective the intervention was not just about pro-Qaddafi forces. According to the early NATO discourse, if rebels attacked civilians NATO would also intervene.

- The second speaker noted the issues around what happened to pro-Qaddafi forces who surrendered to the rebels (danger of reprisals).

Summary:
- Early North Atlantic Council meetings were primarily concerned with protecting the Libyan people.
- There was a general recognition amongst NATO members that there was a need to commit something tangible.
- It was argued that there is a need to move beyond the 'War on Terror' paradigm and towards increased dialogue with Russia and China.
- Civilian protection vs. regime change in Libya was considered.

Panel 4: Syria- a suitable case for intervention?

Political and strategic obstacles to Intervening in Syria
Dr Ian Lesser (German Marshall Fund of the US)

The speaker cited several obstacles and constraints in considering Syria as a suitable case for intervention. Firstly there is a wariness of making new commitments following Iraq and Afghanistan (the notion of 'if you break it, you own it'). Secondly there are limitations on our ability to leverage and shape the situation. Thirdly, looking at the legacy of previous interventions in EU and US foreign policy, even where an operation may be 'over' there is a public and political perception that these interventions are open ended. Lastly despite wide support for responsibility to protect, the extent of support goes down when applied to a specific case like Syria.

In terms of the dynamics within Syria itself, there are certain constraints to international action. The speaker argued that there is currently an impasse in the highly complex situation in Syria and that it is difficult to see a clear winner. Should you choose to support one group it is unclear what you would get from your chosen party. Regionally, within the context of the Arab revolutions the speaker noted a wariness of what can be achieved in Syria due to the longevity of the conflict.

In terms of regional and international constraints the speaker also argued that a possible argument for intervention is to limit the spill over into Lebanon and Iraq. On the other hand the dangers of intervention are numerous (even Turkey is careful how they sit on the situation). The speaker argued that there is a need to consider the costs of engaging contrary to the position of Russia due to their relationship with Syria and the Assad regime.

Syria: the case for intervention
Dr Alan Mendoza (Henry Jackson Society)

The speaker indicated the importance of the negative impact that delaying intervention can have. A year ago the situation in Syria appeared much simpler, there was a clearer picture as the rebels had not yet become so split and divided (in contrast to the highly complex situation that exists now). The longer we leave a problem, the worse it becomes and the more reasons emerge for why we should not intervene. The speaker argued that while we should have acted sooner we need to consider why we should intervene now.

Justifications given for not intervening include the following: We would not know whom we were arming, there is a danger of the conflict spilling over and there would be heightened levels of violence that would accompany arming the rebels. The speaker argued that these may be given as reasons not to intervene but that these problems have occurred anyway. There are issues with refugee flows going into Jordan and Iraq as well as problems in Lebanon. The current situation presents an unlevel 'killing field', with one side heavily armed in comparison to the other.

The speaker argued that the current situation in Syria is a cause for embarrassment for the Western powers. For example, the US said they would not stand by if there was use of chemical weapons but despite production of evidence by Britain and France the US seemingly dragged their feet on the issue asking for more evidence.

On another level, intervention is effectively already taking place. Russia is supplying a flow of arms and providing diplomatic cover at the UN Security Council. The Iranian bankrolling of the Assad regime also contributes men, arms and money to the cause, heightening the unlevel 'killing field' as mentioned previously. It is at this stage in the conflict that the language of the Responsibility to Protect is coming to the fore.

In terms of possible outcomes to the conflict, the speaker argued that if Assad lost, a Sunni regime would come to power and the connection to Hezbollah would be lost. The Iranian influence would also be hit hard and could be reflected in Iraq. In relation to Russia's involvement the loss of Syria would, expose them as a 'paper tiger'.

If the above is true, the speaker argued that it is in western interests to have a weakened Iran and Hezbollah. There may also be implications for Hezbollah in Lebanon should the Assad regime fall.

The speaker noted that we have allowed Assad to keep pushing the line; there is impunity for Hezbollah operatives, indiscriminate killing and now the use of chemical weapons. With Assad closing his vice on the rebels, it does not present a good situation from which to start a peace settlement negotiation. We need to level the playing field to facilitate a negotiated settlement. The speaker claimed that we should therefore intervene and use strategies such as a No-fly-zone and the arming of the rebels to achieve this.

At this stage the speaker pointed out that the reason Islamist rebels are so popular at present is due to their arms advantage (as they are supplied by countries such as Qatar). The speaker argued that had we intervened earlier on it would have been the moderates that we could step in and arm, making them the viable group for overthrowing the regime rather than the Islamists.

Discussion

- It was noted that the majority of Alawites are behind Assad. There is therefore a very strong constituency that would support the regime (due to fear of what would happen to this group should the regime fall).

- The dangers of intervention are numerous. One participant argued that Iran has penetrated every level of the Assad regime, e.g. training indigenous Syrian forces for a war of attrition. Intervention in Syria would also mean that the instability of Lebanon, and Iraq would be heightened.

- A participant noted that the consideration of public opinion within the debate is needed.

- It was argued that one political consideration of intervention is that there would be no sure solution with the rebels taking over. Due to the fact that the rebels are so divided, some kind of joint agreement would need to be made.

- It was noted that the longer you leave it the greater the issue of radical Islamists becomes.

- There is a question as to what the intervention in Syria would look like militarily. The second speaker argued that you could look to air operations amongst other approaches. Libya could be used as an example of what could be done militarily.

- Problems with intervention are argued to be on the political level. We need to consider what comes after the military campaign.

- The ability of military intervention to produce long-term success is questioned.

- The importance of the strategic context is noted with the disengagement from Afghanistan and interventions elsewhere. Overall, there is a series of contingencies moving towards a desire for 'lower maintenance' foreign and security policy.

- A participant mentioned the need to take account of the ethnic and religious diversity (e.g. Kurds) in Syria.

- The role of the NATO air strikes in forcing the hand in the Bosnian conflict was mentioned. There was a question from the floor as to whether Bosnia can be used as an example of successful/ positive intervention? The second speaker argued that Bosnia worked in the sense that issues are being tackled through political means rather than through violence.

- Discussion moved to the responsibility to rebuild. It was argued that this depends on the nature of the intervention. In Libya, for example, it was not implied that there was a responsibility to rebuild. It was considered by one participant whether the responsibility should be more to support liberal democratic forces where possible.

- Could Assad go quietly? Speaker argued that this may be possible, but the problem lies with the rest of the group who are part of the regime (they cannot leave so conveniently).

- Turkey cited as being indispensible to any policy on Syria. Due to their presence, and treaty obligations, Turkey is intimately involved and connected. The possibility of NATO's Article 5 being invoked should the conflict spill over into Turkey was also noted.

- The use of the Bosnian example as a comparison to Syria by the second speaker was argued to break down in terms of the trigger and the will to rebuild in Bosnia. There is in the case of Syria no appetite for a massive rebuilding commitment.

- The first speaker noted that the Israeli debate on intervention is very different. It is more focused on arms, regional balance and what can reach them rather than the humanitarian concerns. The possible consequences of a loss of tolerance by Israel were also considered.

- What are the alternatives to a no fly zone/ is a no-fly zone a solution? Speaker argued that a no-fly zone may not solve conflict but can act as a building block and provide protection for humanitarian operations.

Summary:
- There is a wariness of new commitments following Afghanistan/Iraq and the dynamics in Syria itself present certain constraints to international action.
- Divisions between the rebels and the role of radical Islamists have made the situation more complex.
- It was argued that there is a need to level the 'killing field' through arming the rebels to allow a negotiated settlement. In the present situation Assad's position is too strong to facilitate this.

Final Roundtable: Future Directions for R2P

Professor David Fisher (King's College London)

The speaker argued that the change in the norm of non-intervention was crystallised in the 2005 R2P framework adopted in the UN General Assembly. It advanced the case for non-consensual humanitarian intervention. Historical changes see trends towards over-intervention/ never intervening; these periods of extremes need to be avoided.

The reasons why R2P was adopted are still valid, for example, the memory of Rwanda. The speaker cited Libya, Sierra Leone and Kosovo as 'good' interventions, and argued that the moral case for intervention still remains strong.

There is a need for modest ends by modest means and the responsibility to rebuild may have become an inflated demand. R2P is worth protecting but it is not inevitable that we will. A restatement of the case for humanitarian intervention is important.

Professor Mary Kaldor (London School of Economics)

The speaker began by questioning why 10 years after R2P there is no serious debate on intervening to protect people in Syria. Bosnia played a big role in establishing the norms and narrative of R2P. There was real movement around Bosnia in the work of humanitarian groups. A lot of important ideas, therefore, came out of Bosnia (e.g. establishing war crimes) even if they were not implemented at that point.

The speaker identified a need to draw a distinction between intervention in Afghanistan and Iraq and humanitarian intervention. There was polarisation following Afghanistan/Iraq. For example, liberal interventionists gained scepticism of the use of military means with the fear that this kind of intervention will bring the 'wrong' consequences. This in turn may have pushed liberal interventionists to a more non-interventionist stance.

The association of intervention with military means can be separated. For example, Hugo Grotius was against armed intervention but in favour of humanitarian intervention. The speaker argued that the reluctance to intervene in Syria is due to nervousness following the legacy of Afghanistan/Iraq. One of the consequences of violent regime change is that power goes to armed rebels or a military faction rather than being popular peaceful political change.

The speaker argued that it is necessary to think about Syria in humanitarian terms rather than geopolitical ones. An intervention should be aimed at helping people and de-escalating violence rather than winning and losing. The creation of a protected zone in the liberated areas would be a positive move (with towns being able to negotiate free zone status from the civil war). This would ideally be based around negotiations and UN involvement rather than unilateral action as had been discussed earlier in the conference.

The language of R2P was, in the speaker's view, a mistake. It was argued that the language used for R2P was too top down focused. Instead the language of human security should have been used, e.g. the 'right to be protected'.

The speaker concluded that a process is needed for the whole Middle East to de-escalate violence using a human rights based foreign policy.

Discussion:

- The dilemma in analysing the security situation was noted. It was argued that there appears to be no answer to this from either the humanitarian or realist perspectives.
- It was noted by one participant that it would take a generation before the UK as a nation are prepared to put boots on the ground following Afghanistan and Iraq. There is a perception that in Syria we risk emulating the situations in these countries, and the problems experienced with achieving democracy.
- The responsibility of the Arab League to do something within their region was questioned. For example, Saudi Arabia, Turkey and Jordan are all armed countries that could intervene. If, on the other hand, the West intervene or lead in an intervention you run the risk of imperialist associations.
- The second speaker, in response to the above, argued there is hope in the possibility of a joint effort between Turkey and the Europeans for example.
- A participant argued that there was a failure in following up on Operation Unified Protector with assistance to the very fragile Libyan government (disarmament of militia groups etc) in terms of long-term stabilisation.

- There was a concern that interventions are about counter-terrorism rather than conflict prevention and humanitarian issues.

- It was pointed out that it is possible that an expectation of international intervention has been created by R2P. We could then question whether this fuelled civil war in Syria, with rebels expecting a western reaction. If we follow this line then there is an expectation on western/European states when we do not actually have the capacity or the will to act. You could therefore argue that R2P has a certain responsibility to carry for this situation.

- The second speaker disagreed with the above in terms of the rebels trying to provoke western reaction. The idea of R2P is the movement to a more law-governed world. One of the problems with R2P is they didn't put enough effort into the 'how'.

- The first speaker highlighted the need to recapture the debate for humanitarian intervention and set more modest/ achievable aims.

- One participant pointed out that there was a difficulty in walking away from Iraq due to the humanitarian element.

- A participant argued that if you are going to act it needs to be done decisively. Taking a softer partially committed approach may give the message to rebels that they will get some support but at the same time will tell the regime in question that you will not commit full force.

- Finally the second speaker noted that Iraq discredited intervention as it meant it became mixed up with the 'war on terror'.

Summary:

- There may be a need for a restatement of the case for humanitarian intervention (following Afghanistan/Iraq), with modest ends and modest means.
- It was argued that we need a human rights based foreign policy for the Middle East to de-escalate violence.
- A distinction needs to be drawn between Afghanistan/Iraq and humanitarian intervention (it became mixed up with the 'war on terror') and we need to consider Syria in humanitarian terms rather than geopolitical ones.